*The Sepher Yetzirah
and the Qabalah*

By Manly P. Hall

ISBN: 978-1-63118-481-9

Esoteric Classics:
Studies in Kabbalah

Other Books in this Series and Related Titles

Qabbalistic Teachings and the Tree of Life by M P Hall (978-1-63118-482-6)

The Kabbalah of Masonry & Related Writings by E Levi &c (978-1-63118-453-6)

Fortune-Telling with Dice by Astra Cielo (978-1-63118-466-6)

History, Analysis and Secret Tradition of the Tarot by Hall &c (978-1-63118-445-1)

The Ceremony of Initiation: Analysis & Commentary (978-1-63118-473-4)

Crystal Vision Through Crystal Gazing by Achad (978-1-63118-455-0)

Ancient Mysteries and Secret Societies by M P Hall (978-1-63118-410-9)

The Secrets of Enoch by Enoch (978-1-63118-449-9)

The Path of Light: A Manual of Maha-Yana Buddhism (978-1-63118-471-0)

The Rosicrucian Chemical Marriage by Christian Rosenkreuz (978-1-63118-458-1)

Ghosts in Solid Form by Gambier Bolton (978-1-63118-469-7)

American Indian Freemasonry by A C Parker (978-1-63118-460-4)

The Mysteries of Freemasonry & the Druids by M P Hall &c (978-1-63118-444-4)

Psalms of Solomon by King Solomon (978-1-63118-439-0)

Arcane Formulas or Mental Alchemy by W W Atkinson (978-1-63118-459-8)

The Machinery of the Mind by Dion Fortune (978-1-63118-451-2)

The Gospel of the Nativity of Mary by St. Matthew (978-1-63118-448-2)

Buddhist Psalms by Shinran (978-1-63118-465-9)

The Leadbeater Reader: A Selection of Occult Essays (978-1-63118-483-3)

Alchemy in the Nineteenth Century by H P Blavatsky (978-1-63118-446-8)

The Human Aura: Astral Colors and Thought Forms (978-1-63118-419-2)

Audio versions are also available on Audible, Amazon and Apple

Table of Contents

Introduction...7

Prologue...9

The Sepher Yetzirah:
The Book of Formation

Chapter One...17

Chapter Two...23

Chapter Three...25

Chapter Four...27

Chapter Five...31

Chapter Six...35

INTRODUCTION

The word "esoteric" can be difficult to define. Esotericism in general can be seen less as a system of beliefs and more as a category, which encompasses numerous, different systems of beliefs. It's a bit of juxtaposition, since the word "esoteric" indicates something that few people know about, while the term itself broadly covers numerous philosophies, practices, areas of study and belief systems.

In a greater sense, Esotericism acts as a storehouse for secret knowledge, which is often considered ancient (by *tradition, if not by fact)*, passed down from generation to generation, in private. At various times in history, simply possessing the knowledge of some of these subjects, was considered illegal and a jailable offence, if discovered. This usually included such general topics as Alchemy, Qabalah, Hermeticism, Occultism, Ceremonial Magic, Astrology, Divination, Rosicrucianism and so on. Collectively, these areas of study were often referred to as the esoteric sciences.

Sometimes, the outer garment of a subject isn't esoteric, while what is hidden beneath it, is. As an example, Freemasonry isn't necessarily esoteric by nature (at *least not anymore)*, but certain signs, passwords and handshakes given to the candidate during their initiation, are in fact, esoteric, in the sense that they are hidden from the general public.

Today, in the twenty-first century, such topics are readily available at bookstores across the country, and numerous mainsteam publishers offer beginners guides and coffee-table volumes on many of these subjects, intended for mass appeal. Books like *"The Secret"* have turned previously arcane topics into household knowledge. All that being the case, however, it isn't to say that there still aren't buried secrets to uncover, ancient wisdom being ignored and forgotten mysteries to be explored. In fact, it is often that we are only able to further our own studies by standing on the shoulders of these disappearing giants.

Lamp of Trismegistus is doing its part to help preserve humanity's esoteric history by making some of these classics available to those students who are seeking to unearth the knowledge of these ancient colossi.

So, be sure to check other titles from our *Esoteric Classics* series, as well as our *Occult Fiction*, *Theosophical Classics*, *Foundations of Freemasonry Series*, *Supernatural Fiction*, *Paranormal Research Series*, *Studies in Buddhism* and our *Christian Apocrypha Series*. You can also download the audio versions of most of these titles from Amazon, Apple or Audible, for learning on the go.

PROLOGUE:

THE QABALAH

Albert Pike, quoting from *Transcendental Magic*, thus sums up the importance of Qabbalism as a key to Masonic esotericism: "One is filled with admiration, on penetrating into the Sanctuary of the Kabbalah, at seeing a doctrine so logical, so simple, and at the same time so absolute. The necessary union of ideas and signs, the consecration of the most fundamental realities by the primitive characters; the Trinity of Words, Letters, and Numbers; a philosophy simple as the alphabet, profound and infinite as the Word; theorems more complete and luminous than those of Pythagoras; a theology summed up by counting on one's fingers; an Infinite which can be held in the hollow of an infant's hand; ten ciphers and twenty-two letters, a triangle, a square, and a circle,--these are all the elements of the Kabbalah. These are the elementary principles of the written Word, reflection of that spoken Word that created the world!"

Hebrew theology was divided into three distinct parts. The first was the *law*, the second was *the soul of the law*, and the third was *the soul of the soul of the law*. The law was taught to all the children of Israel; the *Mishna*, or the soul of the law, was revealed to the Rabbanim and teachers; but the *Qabbalah*, the soul of the soul of the law, was cunningly concealed, and only the highest initiates among the Jews were instructed in its secret principles.

According to certain Jewish mystics, Moses ascended Mount Sinai three times, remaining in the presence of God forty days each time. During the first forty days the tables of the written law were delivered to the prophet; during the second forty days he received the soul of the law; and during the last forty days God instructed him in the mysteries of the Qabbalah, the soul of the soul of the law. Moses concealed in the first four books of the Pentateuch the secret instructions that God had given him, and for centuries students of Qabbalism have sought therein the secret doctrine of Israel. As the spiritual nature of man is concealed in his physical body, so the unwritten law--the *Mishna* and the *Qabbalah--is* concealed within the written teachings of the Mosaic code. *Qabbalah* means the *secret or hidden tradition, the unwritten law,* and according to an early Rabbi, it was delivered to man in order that through the aid of its abstruse principles he might learn to understand the mystery of both the universe about him and the universe within him.

The origin of Qabbalism is a legitimate subject for controversy. Early initiates of the Qabbalistic Mysteries believed that its principles were first taught by God to a school of His angels before the fall of man. The angels later communicated the secrets to Adam, so that through the knowledge gained from an understanding of its principles, fallen humanity might regain its lost estate. The Angel Raziel was dispatched from heaven to instruct Adam in the mysteries of the Qabbalah. Different angels were employed to initiate the succeeding patriarchs in this difficult science. Tophiel was the teacher of Shem, Raphael of Isaac, Metatron of Moses, and

Michael of David.

Christian D. Ginsburg has written: "From Adam it passed over to Noah, and then to Abraham, the friend of God, who emigrated with it to Egypt, where the patriarch allowed a portion of this mysterious doctrine to ooze out. It was in this way that the Egyptians obtained some knowledge of it, and the other Eastern nations could introduce it into their philosophical systems. Moses, who was learned in all the wisdom of Egypt, was first initiated into it, in the land of his birth, but became most proficient in it during his wanderings in the wilderness, when he not only devoted to it the leisure hours of the whole forty years, but received lessons in it from one of the angels... Moses also initiated the seventy Elders into the secrets of this doctrine and they again transmitted them from hand to hand. Of all who formed the unbroken line of tradition, David and Solomon were most initiated into the Kabbalah."

According to Eliphas Levi, the three greatest books of Qabbalism are the *Sepher Yetzirah,* The Book of Formation; the *Sepher ha Zohar,* The Book of Splendor; and the *Apocalypse,* The Book of Revelation. The dates of the writing of these books are by no means thoroughly established. Qabbalists declare that the *Sepher Yetzirah* was written by Abraham. Although it is by far the oldest of the Qabbalistic books, it was probably from the pen of the Rabbi Akiba, A.D. 120.

The *Sepher ha Zohar* presumably was written by Simeon ben Jochai, a disciple of Akiba. Rabbi Simeon was sentenced to death about A.D. 161 by Lucius Verus, co-regent of the

Emperor Marc Aurelius Antoninus. He escaped with his son and, hiding in a cave, transcribed the manuscript of the *Zohar* with the assistance of Elias, who appeared to them at intervals. Simeon was twelve years in the cave, during which time he evolved the complicated symbolism of the "Greater Face" and the "Lesser Face." While discoursing with disciples Rabbi Simeon expired, and the "Lamp of Israel" was extinguished. His death and burial were accompanied by many supernatural phenomena. The legend goes on to relate that the secret doctrines of Qabbalism had been in existence since the beginning of the world, but that Rabbi Simeon was the first man permitted to reduce them to writing. Twelve hundred years later the books which he had compiled were discovered and published for the benefit of humanity by Moses de León. The probability is that Moses de León himself compiled the *Zohar* about A.D. 1305, drawing his material from the unwritten secrets of earlier Jewish mystics. The *Apocalypse*, accredited to St. John the Divine, is also of uncertain date, and the identity of its author has never been satisfactorily proved.

Because of its brevity and because it is the key to Qabbalistic thought, the *Sepher Yetzirah* is included here, in full. The *Zohar* contains a vast number of philosophical tenets, and a paraphrase of its salient points is embodied in this work.

Few realize the influence exerted by Qabbalism over mediæval thought, both Christian and Jewish. It taught that there existed within the sacred writings a hidden doctrine which was the key to those writings. This is symbolized by the crossed keys upon the papal crest. Scores of learned minds began to search for those arcane truths by which the race should be

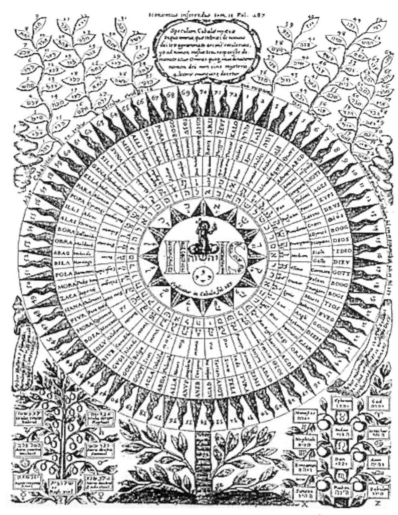

THE SEVENTY-TWO NAMES GOD [1]

redeemed; and that their labor was not without its reward, their subsequent writings have demonstrated.

The theories of Qabbalism are inextricably interwoven with the tenets of alchemy, Hermeticism, Rosicrucianism, and

---

[1] From Kircher's *Œdipus Ægyptiacus*

Freemasonry. The words *Qabbalism* and *Hermeticism* are now considered as synonymous terms covering all the arcana and esotericism of antiquity. The simple Qabbalism of the first centuries of the Christian Era gradually evolved into an elaborate theological system, which became so involved that it was next to impossible to comprehend its dogma.

The Qabbalists divided the uses of their sacred science into five sections. The *Natural Qabbalah* was used solely to assist the investigator in his study of Nature's mysteries. The *Analogical Qabbalah* was formulated to exhibit the relationship which exists between all things in Nature, and it revealed to the wise that all creatures and substances were one in essence, and that man--the Little Universe--was a replica in miniature of God--the Great Universe. The *Contemplative Qabbalah* was evolved for the purpose of revealing through the higher intellectual faculties the mysteries of the celestial spheres. By its aid the abstract reasoning faculties cognized the measureless planes of infinity and learned to know the creatures existing within them. The *Astrological Qabbalah* instructed those who studied its lore in the power, magnitude, and actual substance of the sidereal bodies, and also revealed the mystical constitution of the planet itself. The fifth, or *Magical Qabbalah,* was studied by such as desired to gain control over the demons and subhuman intelligences of the invisible worlds. It was also highly valued as a method of healing the sick by talismans, amulets, charms, and invocations.

The *Sepher Yetzirah,* according to Adolph Franck, differs from other sacred books in that it does not explain the world and the phenomena of which it is the stage by leaning on the

14

idea of God or by setting itself up as the interpreter of the supreme will. This ancient work rather reveals God by estimating His manifold handiwork. In preparing the *Sepher Yetzirah* for the consideration of the reader, five separate English translations have been compared. The resulting form, while it embodies the salient features of each, is not a direct translation from any one Hebrew or Latin text. Although the purpose was to convey the spirit rather than the letter of the ancient document, there are no wide deviations from the original rendition. So far as known, the first translation of the *Sepher Yetzirah* into English was made by the Rev. Dr. Isidor Kalisch, in 1877. In this translation the Hebrew text accompanies the English words. The work of Dr. Kalisch has been used as the foundation of the following interpretation, but material from other authorities has been incorporated and many passages have been rewritten to simplify the general theme.

At hand also was a manuscript copy in English of the *Book of the Cabalistick Art*, by Doctor John Pistor. The document is undated; but judging from the general type of the writing, the copy was made during the eighteenth century. The third volume used as a reference was the *Sepher Yetzirah*, by the late William Wynn Westcott, Magus of the Rosicrucian Society of England. The fourth was the *Sepher Yetzirah*, or The Book of Creation, according to the translation in the *Sacred Books and Early Literature of the East*, edited by Prof. Charles F. Horne. The fifth was a recent publication, *The Book of Formation*, by Knut Stenring, containing an introduction by Arthur Edward Waite. At hand also were four other copies--two German, one

Hebrew, and one Latin. Certain portions of the *Sepher Yetzirah* are considered older and more authentic than the rest, but the controversy regarding them is involved and nonproductive that it is useless to add further comment. The doubtful passages are therefore included in the document at the points where they would naturally fall.

THE SEPHER YETZIRAH:
THE BOOK OF FORMATION

Chapter One

1. YAH, the Lord of Hosts, the living Elohim, King of the Universe, Omnipotent, the Merciful and Gracious God, Supreme and Extolled, Dweller in the Height whose habitation is Eternity, who is Sublime and Most-Holy, engraved His name and ordained (formed) and created the Universe in thirty-two mysterious paths (stages) of wisdom (science), by three Sepharim, namely, Numbers, Letters, and Sounds, which are in Him one and the same.

2. Ten Sephiroth (ten properties from the Ineffable One) and twenty-two letters are the Foundation of all things. Of these twenty-two letters three are called "Mothers," seven "Double," and twelve "Simple."

3. The ten numbers (Sephiroth) out of Nothing are analogous to the ten fingers and the ten toes: five over against five. In the center between them is the covenant with the Only One God. In the spiritual world it is the covenant of the voice (the Word), and in the corporeal world the circumcision of the flesh (the rite of Abraham).

4. Ten are the numbers (of the Sephiroth) out of Nothing, ten--not nine; ten--not eleven. Comprehend this great, wisdom, understand this knowledge and be wise. Inquire into the

mystery and ponder it. Examine all things by means of the ten Sephiroth. Restore the Word to Its Creator and lead the Creator back to His throne again. He is the only Formator and beside Him there is no other. His attributes are ten and are without limit.

5. The ten ineffable Sephiroth have ten infinitudes, which are as follows:

The infinite beginning and the infinite end;

The infinite good and the infinite evil;

The infinite height and the infinite depth;

The infinite East and the infinite West;

The infinite North and the infinite South;

and over them is the Lord Superlatively One, the faithful King. He rules over all in all from His holy habitation for ages of ages.

6. The appearance of the ten spheres (Sephiroth) out of Nothing is as a flash of lightning or a sparkling flame, and they are without beginning or end. The Word of God is in them when they go forth and when they return. They run by His order like a whirlwind and prostrate themselves before His throne.

7. The ten Sephiroth have their end linked to their beginning and their beginning linked to their end, cojoined as the flame is wedded to the live coal, for the Lord is Superlatively

One and to Him there is no second. Before One what can you count?

8. Concerning the number (10) of the spheres of existence (Sephiroth) out of Nothing, seal up your lips and guard your heart as you consider them, and if your mouth opens for utterance and your heart turns towards thought, control them, returning to silence. So it is written: "And the living creatures ran and returned." (Ezekiel i. 14.) And on this wise was the covenant made with us,

9. These are the ten emanations of number out of Nothing:

1st. The spirit of the living Elohim, blessed and more than blessed be the living Elohim of ages. His Voice, His Spirit, and His Word are the Holy Spirit.

2nd. He produced air from the spirit and in the air. He formed and established twenty-two sounds--the letters. Three of them were fundamental, or mothers; seven were double; and twelve were simple (single); but the spirit is the first one and above all.

3rd. Primordial water He extracted from the air. He formed therein twenty-two letters and established them out of mud and loam, making them like a border, putting them up like a wall, and surrounding them as with a rampart. He poured snow upon them and it became earth, as it reads: "He said to the snow be thou earth." (Job. xxxvii. 6.)

4th. Fire (ether) He drew forth from the water. He

engraved and established by it the Throne of Glory. He fashioned the Seraphim, the Ophanim, and the Holy Living Creatures (Cherubim), as His ministering angels; and with (of) these three He formed His habitation, as it reads: "Who made His angels spirits, His ministers a flaming fire." (Psalms civ. 4.)

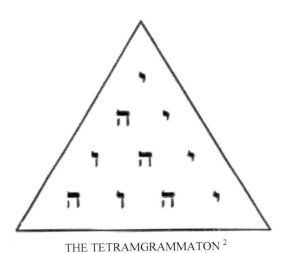

THE TETRAMGRAMMATON [2]

---

[2] By arranging the four letters of the Great Name, יהוה, (*I H V H*), in the form of the Pythagorean Tetractys, the 72 powers of the Great Name of God are manifested. The key to the problem is as follows:

.	=	I	=	10	=	10
. .	=	H I	=	5+10	=	15
. . .	=	V H I	=	6+5+10	=	21
. . . .	=	H V H I	=	5+6+5+10	=	26
				The Great Name of God	=	72

5th. He selected three consonants (I, H, V) from the simple ones--a secret belonging to the three mothers, or first elements; [Aleph, Mem, Shin] (A, M, Sh), air, water, fire (ether). He sealed them with His spirit and fashioned them into a Great Name and with this sealed the universe in six directions. He turned towards the above and sealed the height with [Yod, He, Vau] (I, H, V).

6th. He turned towards the below and sealed the depth with [He, Yod, Vau] (H, I, V).

7th. He turned forward and sealed the East with [Vau, Yod, He] (V, I, H).

8th. He turned backward and sealed the West with [Vau, He, Yod] (V H, I).

9th. He turned to the right and sealed the South with [Yod, Vau, He] (I, V, H).

10th. He turned to the left and sealed the North with [He, Vau, Yod] (H, V, I).

Note: This arrangement of the letters of the Great Name is according to the Rev. Dr. Isidor Kalisch.

10. These are the ten ineffable existences out of nothing: From the spirit of the Living God emanated air; from the air, water; from the water, fire (ether); from the fire, the height and the depth, the East and the West, the North and the South.

Chapter Two

1. There are twenty-two basic (sounds and) letters. Three are the first elements (water, air, fire), fundamentals, or mothers; seven are double letters; and twelve are simple letters. The three fundamental letters [Aleph, Mem, Shin] have as their basis the balance. At one end of the scale are the virtues and at the other the vices, placed in equilibrium by the tongue. Of the fundamental letters [Mem] (M) is mute like the water, [Shin] (Sh) hissing like fire, [Aleph] (A) a reconciling breath between them.

2. The twenty-two basic letters having been designed, appointed, and established by God, He combined, weighed, and exchanged them (each with the others), and formed by them all beings which are in existence, and all which will be formed in time to come.

3. He established twenty-two basic letters, formed by the voice and impressed upon the air by the breath. He set them to be audibly uttered in five different parts of the human mouth: namely, Gutturals, [Aleph, He, Chet, Ayin]; Palatals, [Gimel, Yod, Kaph, Qoph]; Linguals, [Daleth,Teth, Lamed, Nun, Tau]; Dentals, [Zayin, Shin, Samekh, Resh, Tzaddi]; Labials, [Bet, Vau, Mem, Peh].

4. He fixed the twenty-two basic letters in a ring (sphere) like a wall with two hundred and thirty-one gates, and turned the sphere forward and backward. Turned forward, the sphere signified good; when reversed, evil. Three letters may serve for an illustration: There is nothing better than [Ayin, Gimel, Nun]

(O, G, N), pleasure (joy), and nothing worse than [Nun, Gimel, Ayin] (N, G, O), plague (sorrow).

5. How was it all accomplished? He combined, weighed, and changed: the [Aleph] (A) with all the other letters in succession, and all the others again with [Aleph] (A), and all again with [Bet] (B); and so with the whole series of letters. Hence it follows that there are two hundred and thirty-one formations, or gates, through which the powers of the letters go forth; every creature and every language proceeded from One Name and the combinations of its letters.

6. He created a reality out of Nothing. He called the nonentity into existence and hewed colossal pillars from intangible air. This has been shown by the example of combining the letter [Aleph] (A) with all the other letters, and all the other letters with [Aleph] (A). By speaking He created every creature and every word by the power of One Name. As an illustration, consider the twenty-two elementary substances from the primitive substance of [Aleph] (A). The production of every creature from the twenty-two letters is proof that they are in reality the twenty-two parts of one living body.

Chapter Three

1. The first three elements (the Mother letters, [Aleph, Mem, Shin]) resemble a balance, in one scale virtue and in the other vice, placed in equilibrium by the tongue.

2. The three Mothers, [Aleph, Mem, Shin], enclose a great, wonderful, and unknown mystery, and are sealed by six wings (or elementary circles), namely, air, water, fire--each divided into an active and a passive power. The Mothers, [Aleph, Mem, Shin], gave birth to the Fathers (the progenitors), and these gave birth to the generations.

3. God appointed and established three Mothers, [Aleph, Mem, Shin], combined, weighed, and exchanged them, forming by them three Mothers, in the universe, in the year, and in man (male and female).

4. The three Mothers, [Aleph, Mem, Shin], in the universe are: air, water, and fire. Heaven was created from the elementary fire (or ether) [Shin], the earth, comprising sea and land, from the elementary water, [Mem], and the atmospheric air from the elementary air, or spirit, [Aleph], which establishes the balance among them. Thus were all things produced.

5. The three Mothers, [Aleph, Mem, Shin], produce in the year heat, coldness, and the temperate state. Heat was created from fire, coldness from water, and the temperate state from air, which equilibrates them.

6. The three Mothers, [Aleph, Mem, Shin], produce in man (male and female) breast, abdomen, and head. The head was

formed from the fire, [Shin]; the abdomen from the water, [Mem]; and the breast (thorax) from air, [Aleph], which places them in equilibrium.

7. God let the letter [Aleph] (A) predominate in primordial air, crowned it, combined it with the other two, and sealed the air in the universe, the temperate state in the year, and the breast in man (male and female).

8. He let the letter [Mem] (M) predominate in primordial water, crowned it, combined it with the other two, and sealed the earth in the universe (including land and sea), coldness in the year, and the abdomen in man (male and female).

9. He let the letter [Shin] (Sh) predominate in primordial fire, crowned it, combined it with the other two, and sealed heaven in the universe, heat in the year, and the head of man (male and female).

Chapter Four

1. The seven double letters, [Bet, Gimel, Daleth, Kaph, Peh, Resh, Tau] (B, G, D, K, P, R, Th), have a duplicity of pronunciation (two voices), aspirated and unaspirated. They serve as a model of softness and hardness, strength and weakness.

2. The seven double letters symbolize wisdom, riches, fertility, life, power, peace, and grace.

3. The seven double letters also signify the antitheses to which human life is exposed. The opposite of wisdom is foolishness; of riches, poverty; of fertility, sterility; of life, death; of power, servitude; of peace, war; and of beauty, deformity.

4. The seven double letters point out the six dimensions, height, depth, East and West, North and South, and the Holy Temple in the center, which sustains them all.

5. The double letters are seven and not six, they are seven and not eight; reflect upon this fact, search into it and reveal its hidden mystery and place the Creator on His throne again.

6. The seven double letters having been designed, established, purified, weighed, and exchanged by God, He formed of them seven planets in the universe, seven days in the Year, and seven gateways of the senses in man (male and female). From these seven He also produced seven heavens, seven earths, and seven Sabbaths. Therefore He loved seven more than any other number beneath His throne.

7. The seven planets in the universe are: Saturn, Jupiter, Mars, Sun, Venus, Mercury, and Moon. The seven days in the Year are the seven days of the week (possibly the seven creative days are meant). The seven gateways in man (male and female) are two eyes, two ears, two nostrils, and the mouth.

8. *Note*: Knut Stenring differs from other authorities in his arrangement of the planets and days of the week in the following seven stanzas. Kircher has still a different order. Rev. Dr. Isidor Kalisch, William Wynn Westcott, and *The Sacred Books and Early Literature of the East* adopt the following arrangement.

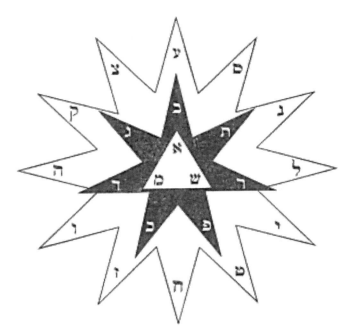

THE HEBREW LETTERS ACCORDING TO THE SEPHER YETZIRAH [3]

---

[3] In the central triangle are the three Mother Letters from which come forth the seven Double Letters--the planets and the heavens. Surrounding the black star are the signs of the zodiac symbolized by the twelve Simple Letters. In the midst of this star is the Invisible Throne of the Most Ancient of the Ancients--the Supreme Definitionless Creator.

1st. He caused the letter. [Bet] (B) to predominate in wisdom, crowned it, combined each with the others, and formed by them the Moon in the universe, the first day in the year, and the right eye in man (male and female).

2nd. He caused the letter [Gimel] (G) to predominate in riches, crowned it, combined each with the others, and formed by them Mars in the universe, the second day in the year, and the right ear in man (male and female).

3rd. He caused the letter [Daleth] (D) to predominate infertility, crowned it, combined each with the others, and formed by them the Sun in the universe, the third day in the year, and the right nostril in man (male and female).

4th. He caused the letter [Kaph] (K) to predominate in life, crowned it, combined each with the others, and formed by them Venus in the universe, the fourth day in the year, and the left eye in man (male and female).

5th. He caused the letter [Peh] (P) to predominate in power, crowned it, combined each with the others, and formed by them Mercury in the universe, the fifth day in the year, and the left ear in man (male and female).

6th. He caused the letter [Resh] (R) to predominate in peace, crowned it, combined each with the others, and formed by them Saturn in the universe, the sixth day in the year, and the left nostril in man (male and female).

7th. He caused the letter [Tau] (Th) to predominate

in grace, crowned it, combined each with the others, and formed by them Jupiter in the universe, the seventh day in the year, and the mouth of man (male and female).

9. With the seven double letters He also designed seven earths, seven heavens, seven continents, seven seas, seven rivers, seven deserts, seven days, seven weeks (from Passover to Pentecost), and in the midst of them His Holy Palace. There is a cycle of seven years and the seventh is the release year, and after seven release years is the Jubilee. For this reason God loves the number seven more than any other thing under the heavens.

10. In this manner God joined the seven double letters together. Two stones build two houses, three stones build six houses, four stones build twenty-four houses, five stones build 120 houses, six stones build 720 houses, and seven stones build 5,040 houses. Make a beginning according to this arrangement and reckon further than the mouth can express or the ear can hear.

Chapter Five

1. The twelve simple letters [He, Vau, Zayin, Chet, Teth, Yod, Lamed, Nun, Samekh, Ayin, Tzaddi, Qoph] (H, V, Z, Ch, T, I, L, N, S, O, Tz, Q) symbolize the twelve fundamental properties: speech, thought, movement, sight, hearing, work, coition, smell, sleep, anger, taste (or swallowing), and mirth.

2. The simple letters correspond to twelve directions: east height, northeast, east depth; south height, southeast, south depth; west height, southwest, west depth; north height, northwest, north depth. They diverge to all eternity and are the arms of the universe.

3. The simple letters having been designed, established, weighed, and exchanged by God, He produced by them twelve zodiacal signs in the universe, twelve months in the year, and twelve chief organs in the human body (male and female).

4. The signs of the zodiac are: Aries, Taurus, Gemini, Cancer, Leo, Virgo, Libra, Scorpio, Sagittarius, Capricorn, Aquarius, and Pisces. The months of the year are: Nisan, Ijar, Sivan, Tammuz, Ab, Elul, Tisri, Marcheshvan, Kislev, Tebet, Sebat, and Adar. The organs of the human body are: two hands, two feet, two kidneys, gall, small intestine, liver, esophagus, stomach, and spleen.

5. *Note*: In the following twelve stanzas, Knut Stenring again differs, this time as to the arrangement of properties:

> *1st.* God caused the letter [He] (H) to predominate in speech, crowned it, combined it with the others, and

fashioned by them Aries (the Ram) in the universe, the month Nisan in the year, and the right foot of the human body (male and female).

2nd. He caused the letter [Vau] (V) to predominate in thought, crowned it, combined it with the others, and fashioned by them Taurus (the Bull) in the universe, the month Ijar in the year, and the right kidney of the human body (male and female).

3rd. He caused the letter [Zayin] (Z) to predominate in movement, crowned it, combined it with the others, and fashioned by them Gemini (the Twins) in the universe, the month Sivan in the year, and the left foot of the human body (male and female).

4th. He caused the letter [Chet] (Ch) to predominate in sight, crowned it, combined it with the others, and fashioned by them Cancer (the Crab) in the universe, the month Tammuz in the year, and the right hand of the human body (male and female).

5th. He caused the letter [Tau] (T) to predominate in hearing, crowned it, combined it with the others, and fashioned by them Leo (the Lion) in the universe, the month Ab in the year, and the left kidney of the human body (male and female).

6th. He caused the letter [Yod] (I) to predominate in work, crowned it, combined it with the others, and fashioned by them Virgo (the Virgin) in the universe, the month Elul in the year, and the left hand of the human body (male and female).

7th. He caused the letter [Lamed] (L) to predominate in coition, crowned it, combined it with the others, and fashioned by them Libra (the Balance) in the universe, the month Tisri in the year, and the gall of the human body (male and female).

8th. He caused the letter [Nun] (N) to predominate in smell, crowned it, combined it with the others, and fashioned by them Scorpio (the Scorpion) in the universe, the month Marcheshvan in the year, and the small intestine in the human body (male and female).

9th. He caused the letter [Samekh] (S) to predominate in sleep, crowned it, combined it with the others, and fashioned by them Sagittarius (the Archer) in the universe, the month Kislev in the year, and the stomach in the human body (male and female).

10th. He caused the letter [Ayin] (O) to predominate in anger, crowned it, combined it with the others, and fashioned by them Capricorn (the Goat) in the universe, the month Tebet in the year, and the liver in the human body (male and female).

11th. He caused the letter [Tzaddi] (Tz) to predominate in taste (or swallowing), crowned it, combined it with the others, and fashioned by them Aquarius (the Water Bearer) in the universe, the month Sebat in the year, and the esophagus in the human body (male and female).

12th. He caused the letter [Qoph] (Q) to predominate in mirth, crowned it, combined it with the others, and fashioned by them Pisces (the Fishes) in the universe, the month Adar in the year, and the spleen in the human body (male and female).

6. He made them as a conflict, He arranged them as provinces and drew them up like a wall. He armed them and set one against another as in warfare. (The Elohim did likewise in the other spheres.)

Chapter Six

1. There are three Mothers or first elements, [Aleph, Mem, Shin] (A, M, Sh), from which emanated three Fathers (progenitors)--primordial (spiritual) air, water, and fire--from which issued the seven planets (heavens) with their angels, and the twelve oblique points (zodiac).

2. To prove this there are three faithful witnesses: the universe, the year, and man. There are the twelve, the balance, and the seven. Above is the Dragon, below is the world, and lastly the heart of man; and in the midst is God who regulates them all.

3. The first elements are air, water, and fire; the fire is above, the water is below, and a breath of air establishes balance between them. The token is: the fire carries the water. The letter [Mem] (M) is mute; [Shin] (Sh) is hissing like fire; there is [Aleph] (A) among them, a breath of air which reconciles the two.

4. The Dragon (Tali) is in the universe like a king upon his throne; the celestial sphere is in the year like a king in his empire; and the heart is in the body of men like a king in warfare.

5. God also set the opposites against each other: the good against the evil, and the evil against the good. Good proceeds from good, evil from evil; the good purifies the bad, the bad the good. The good is reserved for the good, and the evil for the wicked.

6. There are three of which each stands by itself: one is in the affirmative (filled with good), one is in the negative (filled with evil), and the third equilibrates them.

7. There are seven divided three against three, and one in the midst of them (balance). Twelve stand in warfare: three produce love and three hatred; three are life-givers and three are destroyers.

8. The three that cause love are the heart and the two ears; the three that produce hatred are the liver, the gall, and the tongues; the three life-givers are the two nostrils and the spleen; and the three destroyers are the mouth and the two lower openings of the body. Over all these rules God, the faithful king, from His holy habitation in all eternity. God is One above three, three are above seven, seven are above twelve, yet all are linked together.

9. There are twenty-two letters by which the I AM (YAH), the Lord of Hosts, Almighty and Eternal, designed and created by three Sepharim (Numbers, Letters, and Sounds) His universe, and formed by them all creatures and all those things that are yet to come.

10. When the Patriarch Abraham had comprehended the great truths, meditated upon them, and understood them perfectly, the Lord of the Universe (the Tetragrammaton) appeared to him, called him His friend, kissed him upon the head, and made with him a covenant. First, the covenant was between the ten fingers of his hands, which is the covenant of the tongue (spiritual); second, the covenant was between the

ten toes of his feet, which is the covenant of circumcision (material); and God said of him, "Before I formed thee... I knew thee" (Jeremiah i. 5.)

Abraham bound the spirit of the twenty-two letters upon his tongue and God disclosed to him their secrets. God permitted the letters to be immersed in water, He burned them in the fire and imprinted them upon the winds. He distributed them among the seven planets and gave them to the twelve zodiacal signs.

Made in the USA
Monee, IL
03 January 2023

24087972R00023